A Guide to
Japanese Origami

FOLLOW THE STEPS TO MASTER THIS ART

TABLE OF CONTENTS

INTRO: HISTORY OF ORIGAMI

Since paper degrades as it ages, an exact timeline for the origami invention is difficult to come up with. It is widely agreed that around 105 A.D., the paper was invented. In China. During the sixth century, the Japanese first used paper. Other cultures were indeed involved in different forms of folding paper, but it was the Japanese who first discovered the possibilities of using paper as an art medium.

THE NAME'S MEANING

Initially, origami was known as orikata (folded shapes). The art became known as origami in 1880, however. The phrase origami comes from the terms oru (to fold) and kami in Japanese (paper). Why this word was chosen is not clear, although scholars have suggested that the characters for this term were simply the easiest to learn to write for schoolchildren.

POPULARITY

Today, since the paper is a cheap craft supply, many individuals are drawn to the idea of learning how to fold origami figures. It was an art only for the wealthy when origami was first performed, however. For religious reasons, Japanese monks have folded origami figures. Origami has also been used at various formal ceremonies, such as the tradition of folding paper butterflies to decorate sake bottles at the wedding reception of a Japanese couple.

In certain rituals, Tsutsumi, folded paper gift wrappers, are used to symbolize honesty and purity. Another example of ceremonial paper folding is Tsuki, folded paper pieces accompanying a valuable gift, as these versions will serve as a certificate of authenticity.

As paper became more affordable, ordinary individuals started producing origami figures for their correspondence as gifts or creating folded cards and envelopes. Origami has also begun to be used as an educational method, as several principles important to the study of mathematics are involved in the folding process.

Sembazuru Orikata (Thousand Crane Folding), written by Akisato Rito and published in 1797, was the first book about origami. This novel, however, dealt more with cultural traditions than a set of instructions.

In Japan, there is a traditional story that says that if a person folds 1,000 paper cranes, one unique wish will be granted.

ORIGAMI FOR KIDS

The father of the Kindergarten movement and a major advocate for the advantages of paper folding in preschool-age children was Friedrich Froebel, a German educator. He standardized the Folds of Life (basic), Folds of Truth (used to teach geometry), and Folds of Beauty as part of the kindergarten curriculum (used for decorative purposes).

Such kindergarten principles started to make their way to Japan around 1800. At the same time, in school environments, German educators continued to promote the cause of origami. In 1919, renowned educator Rudolf Steiner opened his first school in Germany, especially for the children of Waldorf-Astoria employees (for this reason, it later took on the name 'Waldorf School'). In a co-educational environment, using hands-on teaching methods, Steiner's revolutionary style of education centered on the holistic learning of the infant. Origami was a natural match for this model and was an important part of the curriculum for Waldorf. As part of alternative education systems, Steiner's influence can still be seen worldwide.

Over the years, evidence has supported the advantages of teaching children's origami skills.

Physically,

- It strengthens fine motor abilities and, by adjusting the paper size, the task can be made more or less difficult.
- It teaches essential social skills such as patience and concentration and can be customized to be an experience for individuals or groups.
- It also provides an opportunity for Western kids to learn interactively at a very young age about a new culture.

Origami is a wonderful art for children to learn, and from fortune-tellers and cootie catchers to various paper animals, there are plenty of beginner-level projects to try.

> ***To this day, origami, whether or not they know the formal name for it, is an art form performed by children all over the world.***

The ancient art of paper folding, Origami, is making a comeback. Although some of ancient China's oldest pieces of origami have been discovered and its deepest origins are in ancient Japan, origami can also influence today's education. This art form includes learners and develops their abilities sneakily — including better spatial vision and rational and sequential thought.

Researchers have found several ways in which origami can make lessons attractive while offering the students the skills they. Here are some ways in your classroom that origami can be used to enhance a range of abilities:

The geometrics

Origami has been found to strengthen and bring to life an understanding of geometric concepts, formulas, and labels. This is how you can use it in your class (PDF). Students will learn key terms and ways of describing a form by labeling an origami structure with length, width, and height. By applying a formula to a real-world structure, you can use origami to determine the area.

Skills for Thinking

Other learning modalities excite Origami. It has been shown to use hands-on learning to develop spatial visualization skills. These abilities help kids to understand, describe, and develop their own vernacular for the world around them. Find origami or geometric shapes in nature in your class and then define them with geometric phrases.

The Fractions

For lots of students, the notion of fractions is terrifying. In a tactile way, the folding paper will show the fractions. In your lesson, by folding paper and asking how many folds students will like to construct a certain form, you can use origami to explain the principles of one-half, one-third, or one-fourth. To illustrate the idea of infinity, the process of folding the paper in half and half again and so on can also be used.

Solving Problems

In tasks, there is always one fixed answer and one way to get there. Origami gives kids a chance to overcome something that is not prescribed and allows them to make friends with failure (i.e. trial and error). Show a form in your class and ask students to come up with a way of making it. From different approaches, they can get the solution. Know, no answer is incorrect.

Technology of Fun

Origami is a fun way of describing the principles of physics. A thin piece of paper is not very strong, but it will be if you fold it like an accordion. (For evidence, look at the side of a cardboard box.) Bridges are based on this theory. Origami is also an amusing way to describe molecules. Tetrahedrons and other polyhedra have the shape of many molecules.

Researchers have discovered that learners who use origami in math perform better. In some respects, it is an untapped resource for math instruction supplementation and can be used along the way for geometric construction, geometric and algebraic formulas determination, and manual dexterity increase.

Origami is a perfect way to mix science, technology, engineering, art, and math altogether, in addition to mathematics: STEAM.

Origami is everywhere around us and can be an inspiration for kids and grown-ups alike. So, regardless of how you fold it, origami is a way for kids to participate in math, develop their abilities, and help them appreciate the world around them more. Origami is beyond the fold when it comes to making lessons thrilling.

BASICS OF ORIGAMI

With these simple instructions, learn how to make easy origami. It doesn't have to be hard and boring to make origami. There are plenty of figures that are easy to make and enjoyable.

Just follow the step-by-step guide and in a short time, you'll be able to fold something. You automatically think of some complex paper structure when you think of origami, which is difficult to fold, but it doesn't have to be that way.

WHAT ARE THE PRIMARY FOLDS AND ORIGAMI BASES?

The primary folds are known as Mountain and Valley folds in origami. By folding the top edge down so that the paper adopts a mountain shape, the former is formed. The valley fold instead requires pushing the bottom edge up. The pleat, which is a valley fold followed by a mountain fold that creates a concertina effect, is another significant fold.

The reverse folds, of which there are two forms, are another type of fold to understand: inside and outside. Reverse folds are also used to create the head or tail of an animal.

Bases are a short sequence of folds that, depending on the end target, can then be formed in several directions.

The most popular bases when first studying origami is preliminary, bird, and water bomb, although there are several others. The preliminary base is used in most traditional origami, such as tulip, hydrangea, star box, iris, etc., as its name indicates. It becomes the bird base with a minor adjustment, which is used to build the crane, turtle, and others. In origami, such as the water bomb itself, butterfly, tea plate, and more, the waterbomb base is found.

FOR ORIGAMI, WHAT KIND OF PAPER DO YOU USE?

For origami, several different kinds of paper may be used, but it is important to remember that traditional patterns almost always start with square paper; there are very few models based on any other shapes. It is possible to paint regular origami paper on either one or both sides. Some models do not require double-sided paper, but with double-sided paper, where the inside is clean, the result is much improved. One-sided paper, on the other hand, is helpful for beginners as it can help to envision folding and creases.

Washi paper, suitable for delicate origami models, is Japanese hand-made paper. Chiyogami, brightly patterned paper; Aizoma, which is dyed paper; Shinwazome, raised patterned paper; and Unryu, swirl-decorated dragon paper, are some other paper styles that you may come across. "It is generally recommended to use 6"/15cm, the most common medium format in terms of size.

There are other tools, such as a ruler to help keep creases clean and sharp, that can be useful. To take note of folds, bases, and any other information, a notebook may also be useful.

To help you get the most out of origami, here are some basic tips:

- With clean hands, fold.
- Make sure the square is square,
- Be correct. Accuracy is important because mistakes accumulate rapidly.
- Slow down and take the time to finish a model (it always takes longer than you think).
- Often fold the document away rather than against you, away

from you.

- It is better to fold an edge to an edge than to fold it to a crease.
- Use a larger sheet than normal the first time you try out a new design.
- Turn the paper over to do a mountain fold and do a valley.
- If you ever get stuck with a diagram, refold it with a new board.
- To score creases where you need greater precision when folding, use a ruler and an old biro (with no ink).
- A staple gun makes glue a safe substitute (this isn't cheating!).
- If you build your new model, make a rough diagram of it, however crude or abbreviated, you'll forget otherwise!
- To see where you're going, always look forward to the next painting.
- Do not be afraid to use a model to experiment.
- Save your mistakes, because new, innovative ideas will lead to them.

6 BASICS FOR YOUR TOOLKIT WITH ORIGAMI

Its simplicity is part of the charm of origami. Only crisp, flat paper and two hands of your own, right? Almost. Origami is easy, and keeping it that way is awesome. But, especially when you're just starting, rounding up a few specialized products will set you up for success.

Best of all, you probably have several of these tools or artifacts already around the house that can do the same job.)

1. Paper

The only true origami necessity is paper. There are a few distinct kinds of origami paper, but the regular thin kind (easy to find in craft shops) is ideal for beginners. In Japan, this light, crisp paper is referred to as "kami," which translates simply as "paper." Kami paper is easy to fold and comes in many different colors and patterns (so you can practice, practice, practice, and never get bored!). From leftover wrapping paper to extravagant handmade "Chiyogami" paper, most origami lovers collect all kinds of different pieces of paper. If you're not sure what kind to use, you'll easily find your preferences by playing with various weights and textures.

2. Tools to Cut

Scissors are not used by the majority of modern origami models. Nonetheless, quite a few basic origami designs do contain a few snips here and there. When cutting your paper to the correct starting dimensions, you'll also need scissors.

Many origami models need paper, not just a rectangle, of a particular size or ratio. So it is a must to have a ruler and pencil in your bag. Other cutting tools are helpful, but not necessary, such as a cutting knife with a mat.

3. Tool for Scoring

This tool scores a tidy line without damaging the paper to create a fold. When using thicker paper to make lovely straight lines and crisp corners, this can be super helpful. Specialty scoring tools can be found at most craft supply stores or online. Feel free to use an empty ballpoint pen, a blunt butter knife, or even a knitting needle in a pinch (as long as it's completely out of ink!).

Take your ruler to score a fold and position it where the fold needs to be. Grab and drag your scoring tool over your ruler as if you were drawing a line with a pencil. It's best to begin lightly by scoring, as often that's all you need to create a fold line.

4. Folding Tool for Paper (Bone Folder)

You might be able to get by with only your fingers as tools, depending on what shape you're working on. But a bone folder will be a big help if the origami model is more complex or you have multiple origami models to fold (or you just love being super-precise!).

Traditionally, this tool is made from animal bone, but you can find many that are made of plastic, metal, or wood these days. When flattening a fold, a bone folder takes the place of your fingernail.

You may already have some items, such as letter openers, plastic knives, or clay shaping tools, around your home that can be used as a folding tool. With a smooth, blunt edge, you can use anything easy to hold and knife-shaped.

5. Glue

Although many origamists try to stay away from glue, some renditions of the art form, such as golden venture folding, actually require it. To form larger 3D piece of art, this form of origami connects multiple small modules.

Of course, Glue is also convenient to attach your origami creations to greeting cards or hang them up as mobile devices.

With your origami, a run-of-the-mill glue stick will work wonderfully. If you're glue-averse, you can use double-sided tape, too.

6. Space

Folding origami is more than just a craft for many people; it's also the perfect time to practice mindfulness. The place in which you practice origami is so important because of this.

Don't overthink it. All you need is a nice quiet space with a simple desk and a comfortable chair. Just make sure that you have ample light to see!

Treat yourself to some mental space, in addition to a good peaceful physical space, too. It takes time and practice to learn origami. Your first attempt probably won't look fine, trust me!

The most significant thing is that you enjoy the paper folding process.

Like most hobbies, you can embark on more complicated projects in the future when you perfect the basics of origami. The below shared beginner origami tutorials will help you lay the foundation for mastery of origami.

CRANE

Perhaps the most popular example of origami is the traditional origami crane. A bird base, which is a square base plus two folds of petals, is used. Traditionally, it is said that folding a thousand paper cranes grants you the right to make one particular wish.

One of the most celebrated paper folding projects of all time is the origami crane. It's also the first project to learn how to create initial paper folders until they decide they're interested in origami.

It is so common that the origami crane motif can be seen on drawings, posters, wall decals, trinket boxes, and T-shirts. To symbolize peace and harmony, some people also have origami crane tattoos.

• Collect your supplies

You will need a square sheet of origami paper to fold a typical origami crane. Start with larger documents if you don't have a lot of origami experience. Due to the specifics needed when folding the steps of the crane, smaller sheets are difficult to work with.

Origami cranes look equally folded from patterned paper, but it might be simpler for you to first practice folding the model with a light-colored solid paper. At times, when folding dark or busy patterned sheets, it can be difficult to see the creases. You would need a square sheet of origami paper to fold a typical origami crane. Start with larger documents if you don't have a lot of origami experience.

Due to the specifics needed when folding the steps of the crane, smaller sheets are difficult to work with.

Origami cranes look equally folded from patterned paper, but it might be simpler for you to first practice folding the model with a light-colored solid paper. Sometimes, when folding dark or busy patterned documents, it can be difficult to see the creases.

• Create a Base of the Square

1. A square base starts with an origami crane.
2. Place the colored paper upside down.
3. Fold diagonally in half and open.
4. Then fold the other way around the diagonal in half.
5. On the other page, turn the document over. Fold the document in half, crease, and open well.
6. Then, fold in the other direction once more.
7. Bring the top three corners down towards the bottom of the paper using the creases you have just created. To complete your square base, flatten the model.

• Start the Bird Base

1. Using a bird base, the origami crane is made. A square base plus two petal folds is a bird base.
2. Fold the top left and right flaps into the middle to turn your square base into a bird base, and unfold.
3. To create a horizontal fold that connects the diagonal folds you just created, fold the top of the model downward.
4. Crease well, and unfold, then. Your paper should look like the picture to the left when you are done.
5. Finishing with the Bird Foundation
6. Open the upper flap, simultaneously pressing the sides of the model inwards.
7. Flatten down, well creased. Your crane should look like the

picture to the left when you are done.

8. Turn the model over to complete the bird base and repeat the petal folds on the other side.
9. Fold in the Centre
10. Fold the top flaps, into the middle. Flip your origami crane over, then, on the other hand, repeat this move.
11. Then Crease the legs
12. fold both "legs" of your origami crane up. Yeah. Unfold.

Your Paper Crane Origami is complete

Fold the legs along the creases you just made inside reverse to create a head and tail for your crane. Fold the wings down to finish up your origami crane.

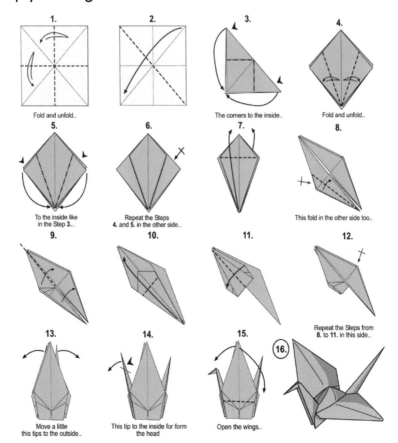

MODULAR BOX OF CUBE

This lovely modular origami cube box, made from six units of Sonobe, is next up. These create great decorations or they can be used as boxes for gifts. They have a pretty patchwork effect if you use several different colored sheets of paper.

PROCEDURE

- **Start if it has one, with your paper white side up**

1. Fold your document from left to right in half and open it. You've got a central crease now.
2. To the central crease, fold the left and right edges and unfold.
3. Fold inwards in the top left corner and bottom right corner, aligning with the previous two creases.
4. Back to the central crease, fold the left and right corners.

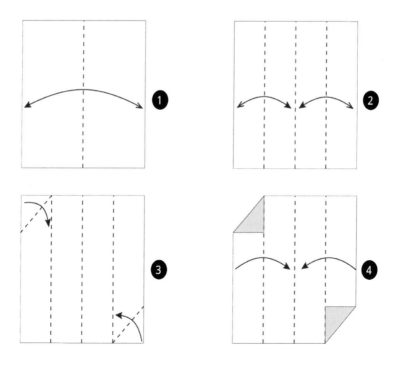

• Create, Rotate, and Repeat Diagonal Folds

1. Fold diagonally up to the right of the lower-left segment along the diagonal flap that is in the right section.
2. Tuck the flap you just built in the right section underneath.
3. Rotate the paper and fold it up in the same way as before in the lower-left corner.

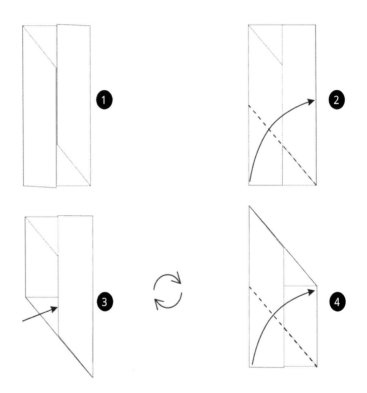

• Link your units to Sonobe

1. Underneath the lower right section, insert the flap.
2. Left to right, flip the model over to the other side.
3. Fold the bottom-left corner up to the right edge's lower stage.
4. Fold-down and to the left of the topmost stage.
5. You need to have six of these units of "Sonobe" now.
6. Begin by bringing one unit to the top and bottom with its flap. Take two more, then bring them to the left and right of the

first one. The two have their flaps out to the right and left on either side.

7. The left one: insert the right bottom point into the central unit's bottom pocket.
8. Right one: Insert the top left point into the central unit's top pocket.

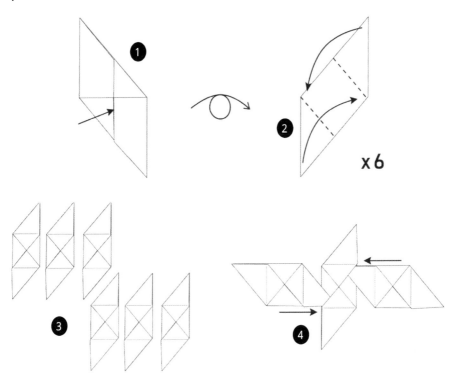

• **Finishing Up**

1. Get two more Sonobe units now and position them above and below the central unit.
2. Insert the top flap from the central unit into the right pocket of the one above.
3. Insert the bottom flap from the central unit into the left pocket of the one below.
4. It's time to pick up the units now, but be careful, they're not

all separated. Form the units into a box, as seen, adding the flaps.

5. You can get the last device and finish the origami cube, now that you have a package.

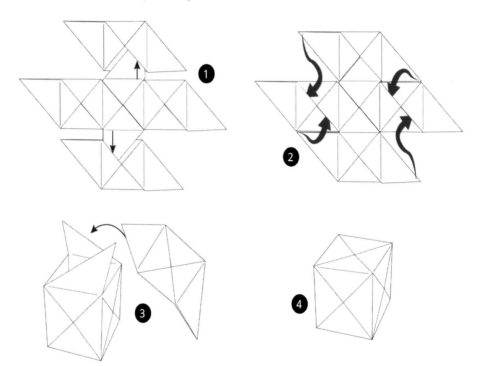

CUP

1. Start with a piece of origami paper that is square.

2. By folding the bottom corner to the top corner, fold the paper in half.

3. Fold the triangle's left edge to the bottom edge, then unfold. We need the crease line only.

4. Fold the triangle's left corner to the end on the right of the crease line.

5. Fold the left corner into the right corner.

6. Fold down the flap at the tip.

7. Turn over the file.

8. Fold the top flap down once again.

9. Again, turn the document over.

10. Raise the pocket open.

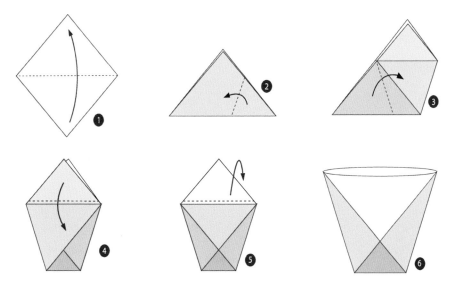

FLOWER AND STEM TULIP

This origami tulip flower has a stem on which it sits as well. For this one, you will need two sheets of square paper. For a handmade origami flower arrangement, make a few and add them to a vase.

- **Start side-up with your paper color**

1. Fold and open the document in half, from left to right. Then, fold and unfold the document in half, top to bottom.
2. Flip the paper to the other page, fold and unfold the paper diagonally in half, in both directions.
3. Collapse down to the bottom of the top, bringing the middle to the left and right edges.

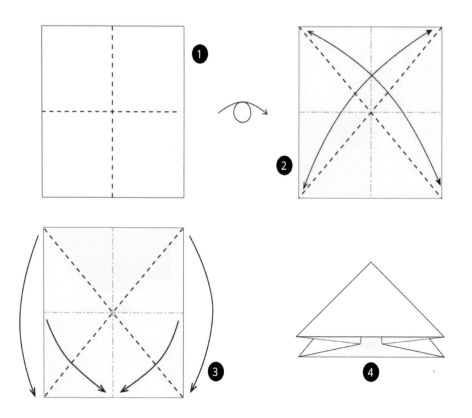

• Continue to fold

1. Up to the top point, fold the lower left and right corners.
2. On the other hand, turn the model over.
3. Up to the top point, fold the lower left and right corners.
4. Fold over the right section to the left
5. From left to right, flip the model over.
6. Fold the right section over to the left once again.
7. Next, fold the front-most flap's right edge just beyond the vertical crease.

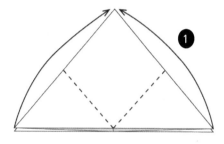 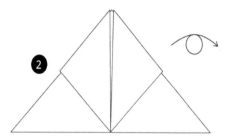

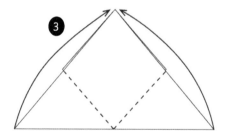 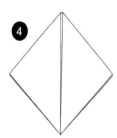

• To make the Petal Base begin to fold

1. On the left section, do the same.
2. Insert into the one underneath the left flap.
3. From left to right, turn the model over and repeat the same steps on this side.
4. Fold up and unfold the bottom part.

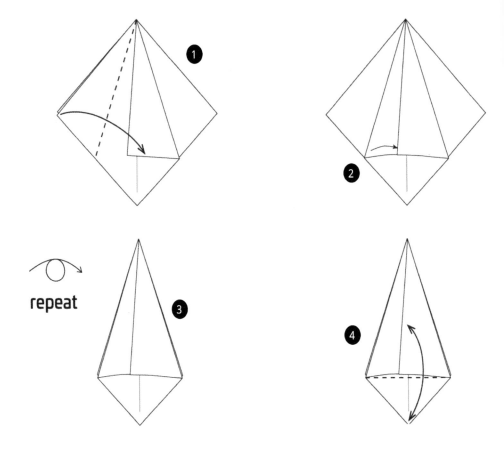

• Shape the Blossom

1. Pick up the model and blast through the tiny hole at the bottom of it. With your fingertips, you can form the flower as it inflates.
2. If the flaps come undone, putting them back in place should be very easy.
3. Peel each petal carefully downwards.
4. Keep the petals peeling until there is a desirable petal arrangement for you.

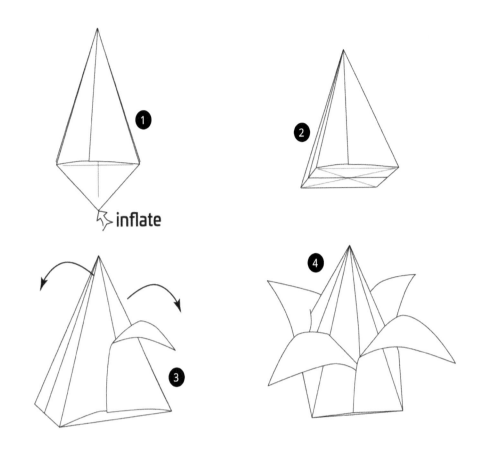

inflate

• Start the Stem Folding

1. Start with the same paper size, this time starting with the white side facing up.
2. Fold the paper diagonally in half and open.
3. Starting with the top point, fold the left and right corners to the central crease.
4. Next, fold the lower left and right edges to conform with the central crease.
5. Fold the lower left and right edges once again to conform with the central crease.
6. Fold the point at the bottom up to the top.

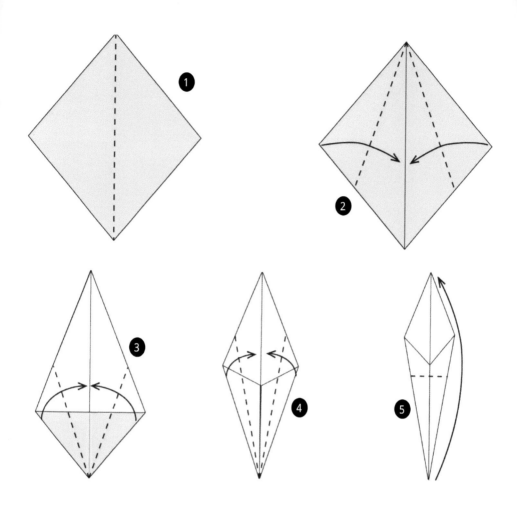

• Finishing Up

1. Fold the model, left to right, in half.
2. Pull back on the larger leaf carefully, peeling it down as you did on the flower with the petals.
3. The stem is finished now, and the thinner stem will now pop into the bottom of the flower. If you need it to remain in position for a long time, you may need to play around with the fit, and use some glue.

WALLET ENVELOPE

This helpful wallet with origami envelopes is simple and easy to make. To keep your cash, or stash store receipts and coupons inside, use the wallet. Use a paper in its favorite color to make it a gift for a friend or relative.

• Folds Beginning

1. In a landscape position, start with your rectangular paper.
2. This is the central fold. Fold the bottom up to the top and make a crease and open. It's going to be where the wallet folds in half. Don't over-create this.
3. Fold the bottom edge upwards, using your currency as a reference. Depending on your note's size, you'll leave a gap here.
4. Fold the feet, along the central fold, upwards.
5. Fold the top down, using it as a reference, over the front sheet. This ensures that on each side, the folds are identical.

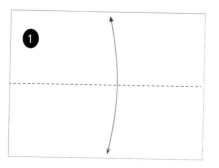
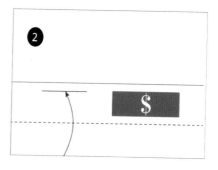

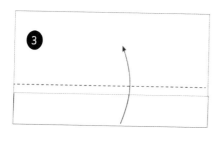
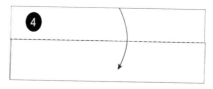

• Continue to fold

1. Back to the start, unfold the paper. To make the outside pockets more durable, fold the bottom flap up a little, around 1/4 inch.
2. At the central fold, refold the paper.
3. Over the front layer, fold the top edge down, using it as a guide. Oh. Unfold.
4. Fold the diagonally inward corners of the bottom right and top right, along the indicated creases.

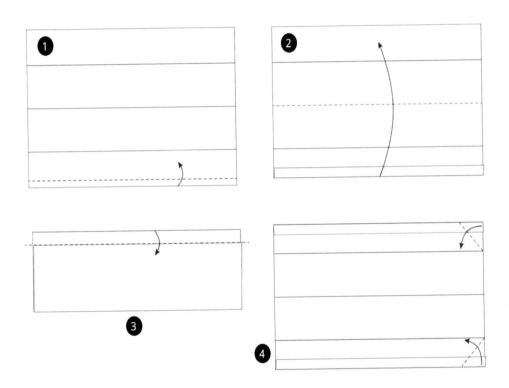

• Finishing Up

1. Refold the indicated creases.
2. Flip the paper over, top to bottom, holding the right side of the flaps you just folded.
3. You can customize how large you want the front pockets on the inside of the wallet by folding less or more. Fold the right end to the left.
4. Fold to the right of the left end and inside the two pockets. You can need to leave a small gap according to your currency note size. Straighten the folds to make sure that all is lined up. You can fold the wallet in half now and it's full.

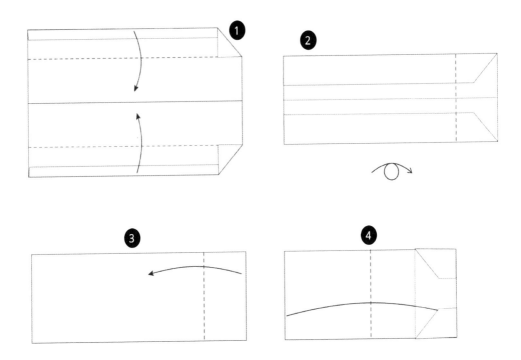

FAN

It couldn't be easier to make these origami fans. For parties and weddings, they're great decorations. With these, you can make little origami earrings as well. Consider making special gifts through the use of richly patterned chiyogami paper for friends.

What I like about these folded paper fans is that glue or scissors are not required: just some paper, markers (or pencils), and imagination. The little ones will have fun folding paper all by themselves and decorating it with shapes, hearts, and doodles.

1. Decorate your piece of paper with the style you like. You can use a pencil to draw it and color it with pencils, pencil crayons, or markers. Decorate for each holiday, if it is for a special holiday, and have one for every occasion.
2. At one end of the paper, start. Fold a one-inch crease and follow it in the opposite direction with another one-inch crease. Repeat this until the paper is folded entirely.
3. Take one end of the paper that is folded and pinch it together. The other end will be left open by this. Just fan out with this ending,
4. Tape up the pinched end to hold your fan together. You can also just staple this section or tie a string around it - whichever you have available.

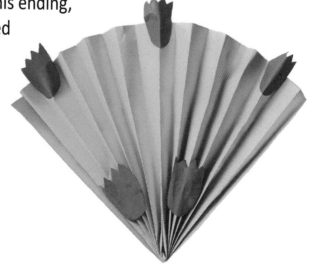

BOAT

For a novice origami project, this traditional origami boat is perfect. It's a lovely toy too, as it can float on the water. Fold several for a kid to create a bathtub fleet. Place a drop of liquid soap at the rear of the boat to make the paper boat move through the water. The boat would be pushed along by the changing surface tension.

What you need: 1 rectangular sheet of paper

• Make Folds of the First

1. Start with your rectangular paper, orient it vertically, going up and down with the long edges.
2. Fold up to the top of the bottom half.
3. Fold the bottom right corner to the left corner and make a slight pinch, just enough to make the paper crease.
4. Open back up with it.

• Build a Triangle Shape

1. Fold the left and right bottom corners up and to the middle by using the crease as a reference.
2. Flatten down the pieces that are folded. Get the document rotated.
3. Fold one sheet along the bottom of the front flaps, from the bottom up.

• A boat starts taking shape

1. On the other page, turn the paper over. In the same manner, fold the bottom edge up.
2. Unfold, then fold in the lower right corner along the crease that you've made.

3. On the bottom left flap, repeat.
4. Shaping the boat's bottom
5. Re-fold back up at the bottom edge. Open the model's bottom. Check around the corners. Flatten and then, under the right part, insert the overlapping flap on the left.
6. Folding Continue
7. Fold up to the top with one sheet. On the back, repeat. Open the model bottom

- The Folds Finalize

Push the left and right flaps apart. Flatten it out, in the form of a ship. Slightly open it. The middle triangle resembles a boat.

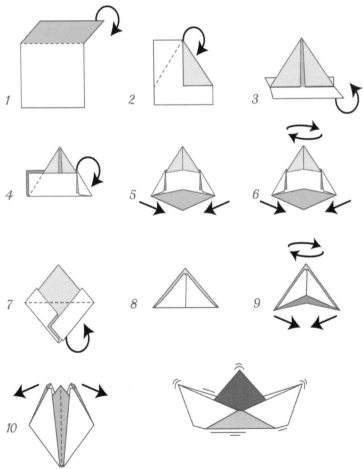

ORIGAMI HORSE HEAD

There are a few folds in the origami horse head that will require you to guess how far to fold and when to stop, as there are no lines and creases to help you. Just go along with the directions and you should be all right, even if the first time it won't come out great.

1. Start with a square, side down, a sheet of origami paper. Follow these instructions to transform it into a square if you only have standard 8.5x11 paper.

2. Fold the left corner in half and position it above the right corner, then unfold it.

3. Fold again in half, but unfold it this time by taking the top corner and placing it over the bottom corner.

4. Take and fold a portion of the bottom corner to the center, then unfold it.

5. Turn over the file.

6. To the crease you just made, fold a portion of the corner.

7. Turn over the file.

8. Here is where a good guess needs to be made. Fold in a portion of the left and right sides, but make sure the creased corners at the bottom do not go through.

9. Using the top of the left and right as fold points, fold the top flap down.

10. As you see in the photo, fold a portion of the same flap upwards.

11. Fold as shown in the picture in the left and right corners.

12. Halve the figure by folding.

13. Draw on the nostrils and the eyes. You've got an origami horse head now.

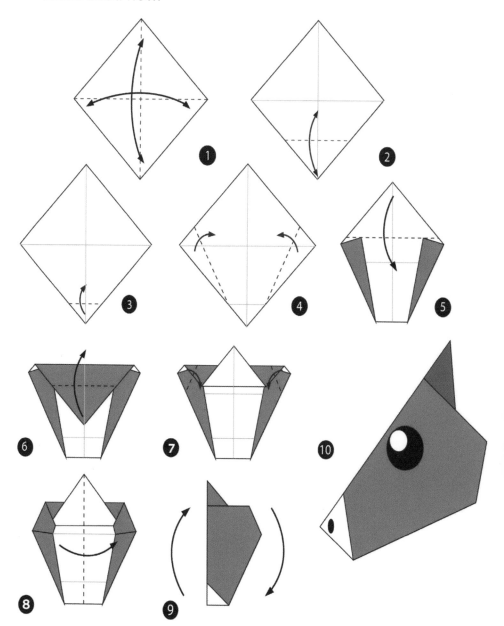

BUTTERFLY

All you need is a square paper and your hands:

1. Fold a square paper diagonally.

2. Fold again along the middle.

3. Fold again in the same way.

4. Open the first fold.

5. Open the next fold.

6. Open another fold.

7. Unfold completely showing the creases.

8. Note the dots, bring those sides together.

9. Crease the fold properly.

10. Fold the right upper layer along the middle.

11. Bring it point-to-point with the top.

12. Do the same with the left upper layer.

13. Make it meet the folded right flap at the top.

14. Turn the paper horizontally.

15. Roll around a finger along the dotted line (don't fold).

16. Fold the top layer over the straight edge (hold with thumb).

17. Flip the structure again.

18. Fold along the crease in the middle.

19. Unfold it again.

20. You now have a butterfly.

 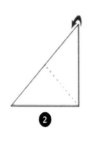

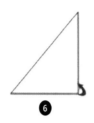 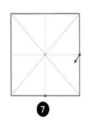 

ELEPHANT

A square paper and your hands are needed:

1. Fold in half to make crease and fold back.

2. Fold forward in the dotted lines.

3. Fold in half.

4. Turn around.

5. Fold in the dotted line.

6. Open as in picture.

7. Flatten as in picture.

8. Cut with a pair of scissors and fold inside.

9. Step fold.

10. Step fold.

11. Pocket fold.

12. Pocket fold and pull out the edge.

13. Cut.

14. Draw eyes and you have an Elephant!

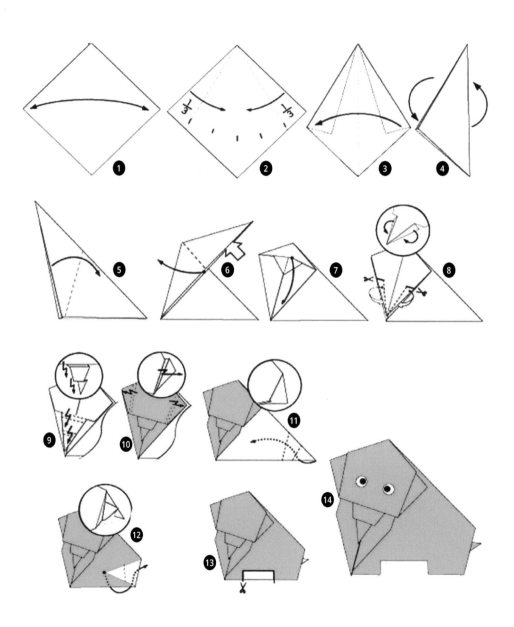

Why not try your hand and make some origami for yourself!!!!

Printed in Great Britain
by Amazon

65997672R00024